Venus

Earth

Asteroid Belt

Saturn

Neptune

Project

Apollo

Ray Spangenburg and Kit Moser

Franklin Watts

A DIVISION OF SCHOLASTIC INC.
NEW YORK · TORONTO · LONDON · AUCKLAND · SYDNEY
MEXICO CITY · NEW DELHI · HONG KONG
DANBURY, CONNECTICUT

To future generations
of space travelers:
The next step is yours.

Photographs ©: AP/Wide World Photos: 62; Corbis-Bettmann/UPI: 16; NASA: cover, 6, 8, 11, 19, 20, 21, 25, 27, 29, 36, 37, 39, 42, 44, 46, 48, 50, 51, 53, 54 right, 54 left, 57, 58, 61, 63, 65, 67, 69, 70, 72, 73, 75, 76, 77, 78, 79, 81, 83, 85 right, 85 left, 88, 89, 91, 92, 93, 94, 98, 101, 102, 105, 106; Photri/NASA: 31, 34; Sovfoto/Eastfoto: 13, 17.

The photograph on the cover shows astronaut John W. Young, commander of the *Apollo 16* lunar landing mission, standing on the Moon.

Library of Congress Cataloging-in-Publication Data

Spangenburg, Ray.
    Project Apollo / by Ray Spangenburg and Kit Moser.
        p. cm.—(Out of this world)
    Includes bibliographical references and index.
    Summary: Describes the planning, development, missions, and accomplishments of Project Apollo, which took the United States to the Moon.
    ISBN 0-531-11761-8 (lib. bdg.)   0-531-13972-7 (pbk.)
    1. Project Apollo (U.S.) —History—Juvenile literature. [1. Project Apollo (U.S.) 2. Spaceflight to the Moon.] I. Moser, Diane, 1944- II. Title. III. Out of this world (Franklin Watts, Inc.)
TL789.8.U6A58183   2001
629.45'4'0973—dc21   00-027089

Acknowledgments

We would like to thank the many people who have contributed to *Project Apollo*. First of all, special appreciation goes to Melissa Stewart, our editor at Franklin Watts, whose steady flow of creativity, energy, enthusiasm, and dedication have infused this series. Our thanks also to NASA Chief Historian Roger D. Launius and Sam Storch, Lecturer at the American Museum-Hayden Planetarium, both of whom reviewed the manuscript and made many valuable suggestions.

For stimulating conversations in the past on the subject of Project Apollo and NASA, many thanks to former astronaut Rusty Schweickart and many NASA engineers, scientists, and administrators. Also, to Tony Reichhardt and John Rhea, once our editors at the former *Space World Magazine,* thanks for starting us out on the fascinating journey we have taken during our years of writing about space.

Contents

An Apollo spacecraft atop its Saturn V launch vehicle

"Sail Out to Sea"

Computer pioneer Grace Hopper once said, "A ship in port is safe, but that is not what ships are for. Sail out to sea and do new things."

It's the sort of code the Apollo astronauts lived by. As astronaut Walter Cunningham recalled in 1999, "We not only believed that we could fly the new spacecraft that they shipped down here, we thought we could fly the crates they shipped them in."

Fellow astronaut Eugene Cernan remembers the days of the Apollo program as a time when the word "impossible" did not exist. After a decade of intense planning and work, it was a time when all the technology the United States needed to go to the Moon was finally in place.

Far from home, an Apollo spacecraft hovers above the Moon.

Going to the Moon was in the air. You could almost taste it. It was a time when people dreamed dreams and built with conviction, determination, and skill. National pride was at stake for the United States, but also, it seemed, were democracy and a way of life.

On May 25, 1961, United States President John F. Kennedy set out the challenge. He said, "I believe that this nation should commit itself to achieving the goal, before this decade is out, of landing a man on the Moon and returning him safely to the Earth." Only 8 years later, the first Apollo astronauts stepped onto the surface of the Moon.

The journeys U.S. astronauts made to the Moon between 1969 and 1972 were dangerous and took great courage. At the time, no one was sure that they would make it home safely. Husbands and wives parted on launch day without any assurance that they would ever see each other again. Children were not sure that their fathers would return.

Space is a harsh and unforgiving place—an infinite, airless ocean where oxygen, food, air pressure, and the familiar tug of Earth's gravity do not exist. The Apollo astronauts were venturing, not just into space, but to the far side of the Moon. Their destination was 239,000 miles (384,633 kilometers) away. No one had ever been that far from home before.

Astronaut Gene Cernan was the last to leave his footprint on the Moon. Looking back 30 years later, he told a reporter that the Apollo missions to the Moon were "probably the greatest singular human endeavor, certainly in modern times, maybe in the history of all mankind." He almost certainly was right.

Chapter 1

The Challenge

The United States venture to land astronauts on the Moon—Project Apollo—began with a few words from President Kennedy in 1961. It was an exciting time. Astronaut Alan Shepard had just completed the first U.S. voyage into space, and the country was buoyed up with the great excitement of this new frontier. Just $3\frac{1}{2}$ years earlier, the first *satellite*, the Soviet Union's *Sputnik 1*, had beeped across the horizon. A lot was happening very fast.

Before 1957, no one had ever succeeded in escaping Earth's gravity to place any object in Earth *orbit*, much less go to the Moon. Based on their calculations, scientists and engineers were sure Earth orbit could be achieved, but no one had yet built a rocket that could do the job.

Just a few weeks after awarding NASA's Distinguished Service Award to astronaut Alan Shepard (left), President John F. Kennedy (right) announced his plan to send astronauts to the Moon.

A lot of people had tried though. In the United States, a rocket scientist named Robert Goddard (1882–1945) experimented with fuels and tested rockets near his home in Massachusetts. In 1926, he fired the first successful *liquid-fuel* rocket. When his neighbors complained about the noise, he packed up his equipment and moved his laboratory to New Mexico. There he continued testing in the wide-open desert areas. During World War II (1939–1945), the U.S. government asked him to develop rocket-assisted takeoff units for airplanes.

In 1929, a Russian theoretician named Konstantin Tsiolkovsky (1857–1935) developed the concept of the *multistage rocket*—a rocket system composed of several rockets. In a multistage rocket, one or more small rockets boost the main rocket in the early stages of flight. After each *booster* has done its job, it separates and falls away. The main rocket doesn't start until the last stage, when the weight of the boosters is no longer part of the *payload*.

By 1945 a team of rocket scientists in Germany had developed a war machine called the V-2 rocket that carried explosives high into Earth's atmosphere and then plunged to its target. It was the most powerful rocket built up to that time.

All these scientists and engineers were looking for a way to overcome Earth's gravity and atmosphere. It was a challenging puzzle. They needed powerful rocket fuels, mighty engines, a design that could soar, navigational control, and much more. Even the German scientists who built rockets for war were originally attracted as boys by the challenge of entering space. Tsiolkovsky, Goddard, and the German rocket team all knew that if they could solve this problem, it would be a great step for humankind. In fact, it would be a leap into a bold, new era—the space age.

Hot Rockets and the Cold War

Then on October 4, 1957 everything changed. On that day, the Soviet Union—also known as the Union of Soviet Socialist Republics (USSR)—launched *Sputnik 1,* the first artificial satellite, into space. The Soviets had done it. They had placed an object in orbit around Earth. Clearly, this feat required tremendous rocket power and a great deal of technological ability.

The Soviet Union launched *Sputnik 1* on October 4, 1957.

The world was amazed and stunned; the United States was in shock. This move by the Soviet Union was a hard blow to American pride. Everyone in the world knew that the Soviet Union and the United States were not on friendly terms. Both nations sought to influence the rest of the world by seeking prestige and showing their strength. The Soviet Union's launch of *Sputnik 1* was highly persuasive. It seemed to prove that the Soviet Union was more powerful and better organized than any other nation in the world, including the United States.

The Soviet Union had formed following the Russian Revolution of 1917 by uniting Russia, Ukraine, Belarus, and several other countries in Central Asia, Eastern Europe, and the Balkan Peninsula. The

On this map, the former Soviet Union is shown in dark green.

Russian Communist Party quickly gained power over the central government, and the nation soon developed into a tyrannical dictatorship. In the years following World War II, the Soviet Union became one of the strongest forces in the world.

Until the union dissolved in 1991, most non-Communist countries viewed the Soviets as an enormous threat to freedom and democracy. By 1957, the United States and the Soviet Union had entered a period known as the Cold War. The Cold War consisted of many hostile and threatening gestures, but few "hot," fighting battles. Each country believed that a "hot," fighting war might break out at any time, though, so they stockpiled nuclear weapons and competed fiercely for worldwide influence and esteem. Both nations recognized that establishing a presence in space could display competence in both science and engineering.

The year 1957 was the International Geophysical Year. Many nations were working on projects to further scientific exploration of our home planet. Launching a satellite would fit nicely with these goals and, at the same time, imply military strength. After all, rockets that could soar into space could also be aimed, with a warhead attached, at any country in the world. No one was likely to miss this political message.

Counter Move

The United States had also been working on launching a satellite, so it wouldn't take long for them to follow the Soviets' lead. But before the United States had a chance to show its own technological prowess, the Soviet Union launched a second, even larger satellite. *Sputnik 2* soared into space in November 1957. In the United States, national dismay soon transformed into fierce determination. The American people did not like being left behind.

U.S. President Dwight D. Eisenhower took stock of his nation's assets before making the next move. Two rockets were nearly ready— a U.S. Navy rocket called Viking and the U.S. Army's Redstone rocket (also called Juno 1). The Redstone had been built by a team of German rocket engineers who were invited to live and work in the United States after World War II. During the war, the team had built the German V-2 bomb used against U.S. allies. Concerned about a public-relations nightmare, Eisenhower chose to go with the Viking.

On December 6, 1957, just a month after the second Sputnik launch, the Viking rocket stood on the launchpad, ready for countdown. Its "passenger" was *Vanguard*, a 6-inch (15-cm) sphere that the

Wernher von Braun (center) and two of his German-born colleagues with a V-2 rocket motor in White Sands, New Mexico.

tall, slender rocket would send speeding into Earth orbit. The count-down ended. Viking roared, lifted a few inches and crumpled suddenly to the ground in an enormous, frightening ball of fire.

Now the United States had to rely on the expertise of Wernher von Braun and his team of German rocket scientists. On January 31, 1958, the Redstone rocket successfully launched a scientific satellite called *Explorer 1*. The United States had entered the space race.

A U.S. Space Program

In October 1958, a new federal agency, the National Aeronautics and Space Administration (NASA), began to work on a very important assignment. It was responsible for running the U.S. space program—a job that quickly proved both challenging and exciting.

By December, NASA announced its first big project. It would send a human being into space. This ambitious undertaking would be called Project Mercury, and it immediately became the agency's primary focus.

Meanwhile, the Soviet Union had not been idle. Before the United States could put its first astronaut in space, the Soviets launched a Vostok spacecraft with a cosmonaut named Yuri Gagarin onboard. On April 12, 1961, Gargarin became the first human to enter space and orbit Earth. Again, the world was amazed, fascinated, and dismayed.

On May 5, 1961, NASA countered with Alan Shepard's flight aboard a Mercury spacecraft named *Freedom 7*. Although the first Mercury flight did not reach Earth orbit and lasted only 15 minutes, Americans were excited. Less than 3 weeks later, President Kennedy proposed that NASA send astronauts to the Moon by the end of the decade. The United States was gearing up for a tremendous adventure.

Yuri Gagarin in the capsule of *Vostok 1*

Chapter 2

Destination: The Moon

The space age had caught hold, and there was no going back. People quickly became dependent on the things satellites could do in space— linking communications, forecasting weather, navigating the oceans, and more. Now, the idea of humans in space had caught the imagination of the nation and the world. Alan Shepard's flight had made the impossible seem possible. Why couldn't humans journey to the Moon?

Much remained to be done, however, and President Kennedy pulled no punches in saying so. No rocket yet existed that was big enough. No spacecraft yet existed to make such a long and dangerous flight. No method existed for landing on the airless, low-gravity surface of the Moon. NASA immediately set to work on many fronts at once.

Mercury: Trying Space Out

First, scientists, engineers, and astronauts needed to know more about getting to space, navigating there, and returning safely to Earth. Also, physicians needed to know more about the effects of space on humans. That's what they hoped to learn from Project Mercury.

Each Mercury mission had specific goals. After Alan Shepard's initial journey into space, Virgil "Gus" Grissom made a similar trip. Then, on February 20, 1962, John Glenn became the first U.S. astronaut to orbit Earth. Three months later, Scott Carpenter flew a similar mission. The last two Mercury flights were marathons—Wally Schirra completed three orbits in 9 hours and 15 minutes, and Gordon Cooper spent 34 hours and 20 minutes in space as he made 22.5 revolutions around the planet.

John Glenn rides into orbit in *Friendship 7*, the Mercury 6 spacecraft.

Gemini: Space Acrobatics

By the time Gordon Cooper returned to Earth, another program had already begun. This one—called Project Gemini—would answer some of NASA's more complicated questions: How do you "walk" in space? What happens when you exit the safety of the spacecraft? How do you navigate a spacecraft to *rendezvous* with another one? How do you *dock* one spacecraft with another? Going to the Moon would require all these skills, and so far no one had tried any of them.

The clock was ticking on Kennedy's challenge to reach the Moon "within the decade." The space race with the Soviet Union also continued to prod NASA to move faster. A week before the first Gemini flight, the Soviets upstaged the United States again. On March 18, 1965, Soviet cosmonaut Aleksei Leonov performed the first space walk. The United States became even more determined to succeed in space.

On March 23, 1965, Gus Grissom and John Young flew the first piloted Gemini mission. The mission went very smoothly. By June, the next Gemini flight was ready, with James McDivitt at the controls. Ed White performed the first U.S. space walk, took photo-

A Titan launch vehicle carries Gemini 3 astronauts Gus Grissom and John Young into space aboard the spacecraft *Molly Brown*.

Astronaut Ed White performs the first U.S. EVA during the Gemini 4 mission.

graphs of Earth from space, and zoomed around in space with a jet-pack. White's *extravehicular activity (EVA)* showed NASA how difficult it is for a person to control movements in space.

Gemini was the first truly piloted spacecraft, and the Gemini flights gave the astronauts their first real taste of what it is like to maneuver a vehicle in the weightlessness of space. The astronauts who flew the remaining Gemini missions practiced rendezvousing with other spacecraft, docking and undocking, and changing orbits. They also performed more EVAs and found out what it was like to live in space for longer and longer periods of time. The *Gemini 7* crew, Frank Borman and Jim Lovell, set an international duration record of 14 days that was not broken for 5 years.

Apollo: Moonbound Limo

While the Gemini crews were walking in space, making rendezvous, and docking spacecraft, many of the scientists and engineers at NASA were looking to the future. A much bigger rocket had to be built and tested. A new spacecraft had to be designed. Astronauts had to be trained and prepared. Landing sites had to be chosen. Everyone working on the program recognized that a voyage to the Moon was a tremendous undertaking. It would require great skill and careful attention to every detail.

Long before anyone would set foot on the Moon, scientists, engineers, and mission planners had to know a lot more about what the surface was like. Had impacts ground it to such a fine powder that astronauts might sink to their waists or even over their heads in the powdery dust? How rugged was the terrain? Could a spacecraft land there? If so, where?

NASA began sending unmanned probes to the Moon very early—in fact the first one, *Pioneer 4*, was launched in March 1959. The Soviet Union also succeeded in landing its first probe in September of the same year.

"Plan A": Straight Moon Shot

At first, most people assumed that NASA would build a spacecraft that would travel directly to the Moon, land there, and then lift off from the Moon and return to Earth. Within NASA, this scenario became known as "direct ascent." However, a closer look revealed one major problem with this plan—the need for immense liftoff power.

Such a spacecraft would have to carry a large booster rocket with it for liftoff from the Moon's surface. That meant the *launch vehicle* would have to lift both the spacecraft and its return booster from Earth's surface. This kind of launch vehicle would be costly, and it would take many years to develop. As a result, the straightforward direct-ascent approach was soon abandoned.

Wernher von Braun, who later became head of NASA's rocket team, began campaigning early for an approach known as Earth-orbit rendezvous. Why not launch separate parts of the spaceship into an orbit above Earth, he suggested, where they could be assembled for the voyage to the Moon? As early as 1952—years before Kennedy's famous challenge—von Braun had written about this idea. It would require much less launch power than direct ascent.

Coming from the foremost U.S. rocket expert, von Braun's suggestion carried considerable influence. He liked the idea because it meant building a space station, which could then be used for other projects. It was a big vision, and it had clear long-term advantages. This scenario became known as "the von Braun paradigm for space exploration."

Unfortunately, von Braun's approach would take a long time to implement. NASA would have to build a space station and then develop a method of assembling the pieces in the weightlessness of space. The United States was in a race against the Soviet Union, and the space-station approach was too slow. International politics won out over logic.

NASA considered several other plans. Workers at NASA's Jet Propulsion Laboratory in Pasadena, California, suggested building a separate return vehicle and sending it to the Moon before the astronauts began their journey. The return spacecraft would be waiting for the astronauts when they arrived. This plan would require two launches, but neither spacecraft would have to carry all the fuel required to transport the astronauts and their equipment both to and from the Moon.

Another proposal suggested sending a single astronaut on a one-way trip with enough supplies to sustain him on the Moon's surface until a return spacecraft arrived to pick him up. Several people actually volunteered for this trip, but NASA never considered the idea seriously.

In another scenario, designers suggested arranging a refueling rendezvous on the way to the Moon. However, NASA saw too many hazards in refueling so far from home.

Finally, NASA began to consider a plan that had first been suggested in 1959. It called for sending astronauts to the Moon in one vehicle. While the main spacecraft orbited the Moon, a smaller lunar lander would descend to the Moon's surface. When the astronauts had finished their observations, the lunar lander would rendezvous and dock with the main spacecraft. Then the astronauts would return to Earth.

Tugboat to the Moon

By 1961, NASA Director Robert Gilruth of the newly completed Manned Spacecraft Center in Houston, Texas, and others had begun plans for the Moon landing. Despite objections by the President's Science Advisory Committee, by 1962, NASA officials clearly favored the lunar orbit rendezvous scenario. Intense work soon began on a three-part spacecraft that would carry astronauts into Earth orbit and then on to the Moon, where they would orbit and land.

Robert Gilruth (right) in 1968 with NASA
Administrator Thomas Paine (left)

This plan made sense in terms of development and operational costs, but it was risky. Transfer and rendezvous would take place in lunar orbit, far from Earth's safety. If anything went wrong, the crew might not get back home. Earth-orbit rendezvous was safer and made sense, but it would take too long. Finally, von Braun conceded that the schedule did not leave room for his paradigm, and he gave in. Lunar orbit rendezvous won out.*

* Some critics say that NASA's decision to go with the lunar orbit rendezvous plan put them in the position of developing technology that could not easily be built on later. As a result, a really functional space station did not begin to take shape until the end of the twentieth century. If NASA had followed von Braun's suggestions, some people argue, a more sophisticated technology might have developed sooner.

While aerospace engineers at North American Aviation Company in Downey, California, began building the Apollo spacecraft, Wernher von Braun and his team at the Marshall Space Flight Center in Huntsville, Alabama, started to construct the huge launch vehicle that would carry the new spacecraft all the way to the Moon. The Saturn V liquid-fuel multistage rocket would make all previous launch vehicles look like toy miniatures.

The Mother Ship's Parts

The Apollo spacecraft had three parts—the *command module (CM)*, the *service module (SM)*, and the *lunar module (LM)*. Think of the CM as the main ship, the SM as the storage shed or baggage car, and the LM as the lunar taxi.

The command module was Apollo's main traveling cabin from Earth to the Moon and back. It was 11 feet (3.4 m) tall and 13 feet (4 m) in diameter at the base. At liftoff, it weighed 13,000 pounds (5,897 kg), including its crew. The cone-shaped crew's quarters also functioned as the cockpit, containing the computer and manual-control instruments. In addition, it had a *docking adapter* that could dock with the lunar module. Compared to earlier spacecraft, it was roomy and included an alcove where astronauts could sleep. There was room in the alcove for stowing gear and a galley containing a varied menu of freeze-dried meals.

The service module was the least glamorous segment of the space-craft—little more than a baggage car. However, it had an important role. The cylindrical-shaped SM carried the spacecraft's propulsion unit, fuel, oxygen, and other necessities.

When the Apollo spacecraft reached the Moon, two of the three crew members would enter the much smaller lunar module. Then this

This diagram shows the three-part Apollo spacecraft. The large cylinder at the top is the service module, with its engines on top. The inverted cone at the center is the crew's quarters, or command module. The strange contraption at the bottom of the diagram is the lunar module.

UNITED STATES

mini-spacecraft would separate from the other two sections of the Apollo spacecraft and descend to the Moon's surface. There, the two-person exploration team would perform EVAs—walking on the surface of the Moon, where no atmosphere would envelop them, no air pressure existed, and extreme temperatures awaited them.

When the astronauts were ready to leave the Moon, the LM would lift off, using its own ascent propulsion system. The descent portion of the LM would be left behind. Once the astronauts had returned to the combined command and service modules (CSM), they would dock and reenter the command module. There they would rejoin their pilot and head back home to Earth.

Tragedy Strikes

All the pieces for the first test voyages appeared to be nearly in place, and the *Apollo 1* launch date was approaching rapidly. Gus Grissom, Ed White, and Roger Chaffee were scheduled to fly this mission. Grissom was a veteran of both the Mercury and Gemini programs, and Ed White flew aboard *Gemini 4*. Roger Chaffee was a new astronaut who had never been in space before. The three of them, with their back-up crew, had worked with the spacecraft during its development. They followed it from production, through assembly, and through every kind of test.

The astronauts were concerned about the mission. In fact, Gus Grissom jokingly hung a lemon outside the command module to show his frank opinion. White and Chaffee felt uneasy too—literally thousands of parts in the spacecraft and rocket had to work together perfectly, and that goal still seemed to be a long way off.

Despite their reservations, the astronauts were reluctant to slow progress. After all, this was a race. National prestige was at stake. Besides, so far, NASA had experienced no major accidents on the launchpad, in spaceflight, or during landing.

On January 26, 1967, astronaut Wally Schirra and the two other back-up astronauts did an "all-up" system test of the *Apollo 1* command module. That is, they performed a dry run without actually launching. The CM was fully powered, but the cabin was not pressurized with oxygen. After the test, Schirra had a bad feeling. In his book, *Schirra's Space*, he recalls saying to Grissom, "Frankly, Gus, I don't like it. You're going to be in there with full oxygen tomorrow, and if you have the same feeling I do, I suggest you get out."

The next day, the official crew boarded the *Apollo 1* command module and began testing. As the long day's tests neared conclusion,

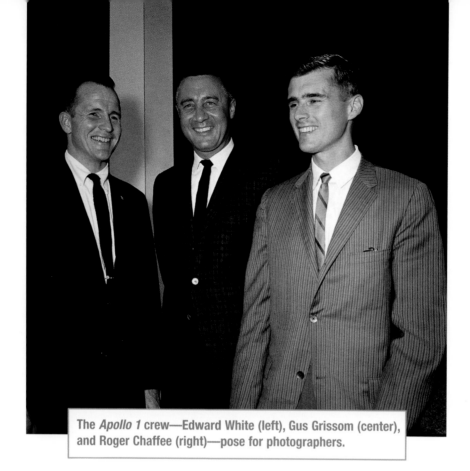

The *Apollo 1* crew—Edward White (left), Gus Grissom (center), and Roger Chaffee (right)—pose for photographers.

the time came to run the test Schirra had mentioned. The atmospheric air in the cabin was replaced by 16.7 pounds (7.6 kg) of pure oxygen. Within moments, technical assistants outside the spacecraft heard a yell over the radio, and then a clear announcement, "There's a fire in here." The voice was Roger Chaffee's, firm and businesslike. Then another voice—unrecognizable, panicked, and indistinct.

It was all over in seconds. From outside the capsule, observers saw a sudden flash of light arc above the capsule. The nearest technician raced to open the hatch but was blown back by an explosion and flying debris. No one could reach *Apollo 1* in time, and all three astronauts died of asphyxiation. They were the first U.S. astronauts lost in a spacecraft.

Gus Grissom was one of the original Mercury Seven, the astronauts chosen to fly in the first U.S. missions in space. He had flown the second Mercury mission, *Liberty Bell 7*, and the first Gemini mission, *Molly Brown*. Based on his skills and experience, he had been chosen to command the first Apollo mission. He is remembered as shy, a little gruff, and a superb astronaut.

In 1965, Ed White, an Air Force lieutenant colonel, made the first U.S. space walk during his 4-day flight aboard *Gemini 4*. His space walk lasted 21 minutes, more than twice the planned time. It was his only spaceflight.

Roger Chaffee was the only member of the *Apollo 1* crew who had never flown in space. Now he would never have the chance. He was a lieutenant commander in the Navy. He lived next door to astronaut Eugene Cernan who remembers him as both a workaholic and a guy with a great sense of humor

Just a few weeks before he died, Gus Grissom wrote: "There will be risks, as there are in any experimental program, and sooner or later, we're going to . . . lose somebody. I hope this never happens, . . . but if it does, I hope the American people won't think it's too high a price to pay for our space program."

Renewed Caution

NASA was stunned and the nation was shocked by the tragedy high above Launchpad 34. NASA and the United States had stumbled. The enormous complexity of sending astronauts to the Moon required balanced, highly coordinated direction and administration, and NASA's critics pointed out that the agency's direction had failed at the highest level. Human lives were lost.

Everything else stopped while investigators probed the causes of the disaster. NASA's investigation was thorough and unrelenting. Everyone wanted answers. What had happened? Why? Could it happen again? How could further tragedies be prevented?

The investigators discovered that a short circuit in the electrical system had caused sparks during the last test. Nearby materials in the

This photo shows some of the equipment and cables charred by the fire in the *Apollo 1* command module.

spacecraft were not fireproof. They burst into flame, and then flashed into an uncontrollable blaze in the cabin's oxygen-rich atmosphere. NASA set engineers to work immediately, redesigning the capsule to reduce the chance of fire and to make an emergency exit possible.

Grissom, White, and Young were not the first astronauts to die—airplane crashes had killed three others. But the United States had never before lost astronauts in a spacecraft. As NASA Administrator James Webb told reporters, "We've always known that something like this was going to happen sooner or later. . . . who would have thought the first tragedy would be on the ground?"

The astronauts who died were brave men, and all three knew the risks. They also knew the thrill of working on the cutting edge. They all had vision and a sense of mission. Grissom believed crewed missions to Mars and space stations built in space would follow naturally behind the Apollo missions. White believed that human curiosity about the solar system would only be satisfied when people could travel in space and see it for themselves. For these three men who gave their lives, the greatest eulogy ever possible would be to go on—to land astronauts on the Moon and to continue the exploration of space.

Chapter 3

Back on Track

Project Apollo recovered slowly from the blow of "The Fire" as everyone in Houston, Texas, and around Cape Kennedy, Florida, referred to the tragic accident. Finally, the design changes on the spacecraft were complete and had been certified. Tests without crews (*Apollo 2–6*) were completed. Now it was time to put astronauts back into space.

Mission planners had laid out four test missions with astronaut crews. These missions would check out all the systems and make sure everything was safe and worked right—before any Apollo mission would ever attempt the primary goal: landing on the Moon. Each of the four test missions would verify a portion of the full-scale Moon landing. Each one would answer the major questions that haunted NASA: Would the systems work? Would the astronauts be safe?

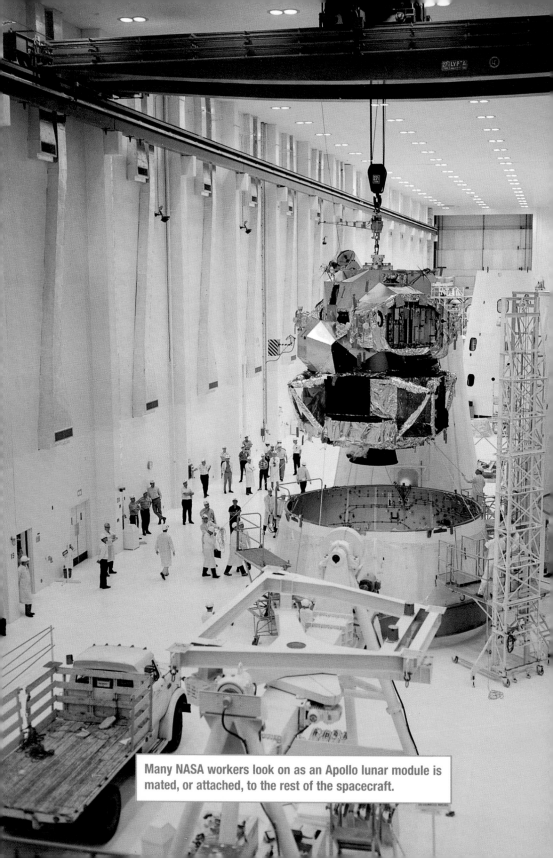

Many NASA workers look on as an Apollo lunar module is mated, or attached, to the rest of the spacecraft.

The Apollo 7 mission was designed to answer the big question raised by *Apollo 1*: "Is the Apollo spacecraft now safe to fly in space?" *Apollo 7* would fly in Earth orbit to test the command module.

Then a decision had to be made. The next mission was scheduled to test the lunar module in Earth orbit, but the LM wasn't ready yet. Meanwhile, NASA program managers worried that the Soviet Union might be on the verge of sending an astronaut around the Moon—if not to actually land on the Moon.

So a bold new plan was born. *Apollo 8*—only the second piloted mission of the Apollo spacecraft—would travel all the way to the Moon. A trip to the Moon would require the big Saturn V rocket, but that was no problem. It was ready, and the mission would be a powerful public-relations coup. It would provide a spectacular display of U.S. readiness—even though the pieces were not all in place yet for a real landing.

During *Apollo 9*, astronauts would test the LM in Earth orbit. If that mission went well, *Apollo 10* would be a dress rehearsal in lunar orbit. The spacecraft would go to the Moon and orbit there, while astronauts took the LM out for a spin around the Moon. This exercise would answer an important question: Is there anything different about operating the LM in lunar orbit than in Earth orbit? It would also be one more dry run to the Moon and back.

First Flight

On October 11, 1968, *Apollo 7* was poised to carry astronauts Wally Schirra, Donn Eisele, and Walter Cunningham into space. The command module cabin was now much safer. Just before and during liftoff, the atmosphere inside the cabin was no longer 100 percent oxygen.

The crew of *Apollo 7*—Donn Eisele (left), Wally Schirra (center), and Walter Cunningham (right)—zoomed into space on October 11, 1968.

During this critical period when fire hazard was high, the atmosphere was filled with 60 percent oxygen and 40 percent nitrogen. Inside the crew's suits, though, the atmosphere was maintained at 100 percent oxygen. After liftoff, the cabin atmosphere was replaced with 100 percent oxygen with a pressure of 5 pounds per square inch (2.9 kg/cm²).

Other new safety features had also been added, including a fire extinguisher, oxygen masks for emergencies, and an onboard television camera. These devices made *Apollo 7*'s liftoff much safer than *Apollo 1*'s ground test.

If Gus Grissom had not been killed in the fire, he would have been the commander of the first Apollo flight. When it came to a "shakedown" flight designed to pinpoint problems and test all systems, Gus Grissom had always been NASA's most trusted astronaut. Instead, the crew's commander would be Wally Schirra, a veteran of both the Mercury and Gemini programs. He had proved himself an excellent space pilot in both of the missions he had flown.

Even though *Apollo 7* had no lunar module aboard, Walter Cunningham would have the title of LM pilot. He was the first civilian astronaut to fly in space. Donn Eisele would be the CM pilot. Eisele was considered the most methodical and introspective of the crew, and his job would be to check out the CM's intricate guidance and navigational systems, piece by piece and item by item.

Naturally, everyone focuses most on the astronauts who would form the crew, but no spaceflight is ever completed without the help of a large team. A ground crew makes sure everything is in order with the many technical systems involved, from rockets to spacecraft, and

From countdown through liftoff, technicians in the Firing Room at the Launch Control Center at Kennedy Space Center in Cape Canaveral, Florida, watch over an Apollo rocket and all its functions.

from computers to nuts and bolts. At Mission Control, experts monitor every phase of the spacecraft's systems during a mission. NASA assigns a back-up crew of astronauts that trains right alongside the primary crew, ready to step in if anything happens. A support team of astronauts is also assigned. Many others work behind the scenes.

All these people are essential to a space mission's success. For the *Apollo 7* mission, the three astronauts on the support crew would keep a flight data file for the mission. They would also set up the cockpit area for countdown tests and work out emergency procedures for various scenarios, using the spacecraft simulators.

Finally, the morning of liftoff arrived. The crew mounted the *gantry*—the tall, scaffolding-like structure next to the rocket. They entered the command module and positioned themselves in their seats. As Schirra later wrote, "It was a telling moment . . . when the gantry was pulled away, and the crew was left alone in its spacecraft atop the booster. This is the moment when we lost real touch with Earthlings, who became voices by radio only."

Apollo 7 was sitting atop the Saturn 1B—von Braun's enormous Saturn V rocket would be held for later flights to the Moon. Even the Saturn 1B first stage was big though. It was composed of a cluster of eight huge engines. Together they had a total *thrust* of 1.6 million pounds (725,748 kg)—nearly 3 times the thrust of the largest rocket used during Project Gemini. The launch vehicle's second stage, called an S4B, produced 200,000 pounds (90,700 kg) of thrust. Schirra described riding under this rocket's power as "like being in an erupting volcano, with sparks and fire and smoke and debris all over the place."

This was the first time a crewed U.S. spaceflight had traveled into orbit on the power of a rocket built especially for that purpose. All the

Mercury and Gemini flights were launched by rockets developed for carrying military payloads. Unlike those flights, which subjected astronauts to as much as ten times the normal gravity on Earth (10 gs), the Apollo liftoff never exceeded 1 g—the amount of gravity we experience on Earth every day. It was a comfortable ride all the way, and the crew could easily watch all the dials and reach all the many panels of switches.

As soon as the astronauts arrived in orbit, they veered slowly around to meet up with the S4B rocket that had just lifted them into orbit and then dropped away. It was orbiting just a little behind the spacecraft. The plan was to rendezvous and simulate docking—even though there was nothing to dock to. This exercise allowed the astronauts to test the maneuverability of the CM.

This photo of *Apollo 7*'s expended S4B rocket stage was taken by astronauts onboard the Apollo 7 spacecraft during docking maneuvers. The white disc inside the open panels is a simulated docking target resembling the one used for docking to the lunar module.

Because no lunar module was along on this trial run, the S4B could take its place as an approximate stand-in. During a Moon landing mission, the LM would be riding on an S4B, and the Apollo spacecraft would move in, dock with it, and pull away. The LM would then ride to the Moon sitting on the nose of the combined command and service module (CSM).

This test did not go as planned, however. One panel of the LM cubbyhole on the S4B did not open. Even if the LM had been there, the Apollo spacecraft could not have reached it. Schirra put this on his list of things that had to be fixed. Next, the crew tried out the powerful CSM engines and discovered that they were, as Eisele put it, "a real boot in the seat." This spacecraft had a lot more zip than anything the astronauts had handled before.

Besides testing the spacecraft, NASA officials had another equally important goal in mind for the Apollo 7 mission. They wanted to gain the support and confidence of the American public. That's why they had installed a television camera in the CM. It could transmit coverage of the mission to Houston, creating a daily 10-minute television show that would be broadcast live from space.

But that didn't go so smoothly either. On the second morning of the flight, the ground controller, working on instructions he had received, insisted that the first television transmission was on the schedule for that day. "We're not going on television today. It's not in our time line," Schirra responded bluntly. The *Apollo 7* crew's job was to check each system, item by item, running down an organized checklist. The television camera was not at the top of the list, and Schirra didn't want to hook it up until its electrical circuit was checked. Memories of the *Apollo 1* CM's electrical short and fire still echoed in his mind.

So, despite Mission Control's objections, Schirra, Eisele, and Cunningham began checking each and every system. The second maneuvering test—an orbital change and rendezvous with the S4B—was going to be tough. *Apollo 7* had no radar to tell them how far away the target was and how quickly they were approaching it. The exercise would have to be done entirely by "feel." The CSM was so much larger than Gemini that Schirra wasn't sure he could slow it down so that it wouldn't collide with the target. Finally, Apollo got within about 100 feet (30 m) of the target. Schirra pulled back, and the three astronauts brought out a bag of hot coffee for their celebration.

By the third day, the astronauts were ready to go on television. "The Walt, Wally, and Donn Show" premiered on October 14, 1968. As Schirra announced, it came to audiences straight "from the Apollo room high atop everything." The show was a huge success.

The Apollo 7 crew had one experience they would have been happy to avoid. They discovered that having a cold in space is even more miserable than having a cold on a high-flying jet. Before the launch date, Schirra had gone duck hunting and got soaked in the cold waters of the duck blind he and his friend were hunting in. By the time the Apollo 7 mission was in progress, Schirra had a miserable cold,

Apollo 7 Crew: Emmy Winners

Wally Schirra, Donn Eisele, and Walter Cunningham became so popular with their television broadcasts from space that the Academy of Television Arts and Sciences gave them a special Emmy Award in 1968. It was rumored that the crew's frequent arguments with ground controllers during the *Apollo 7* mission kept NASA from flying any of them in space again. Schirra likes to point out that he had planned to retire after the *Apollo 7* flight and had announced his decision beforehand. Eisele went on to become director of the Peace Corps in Thailand. Cunningham was a physicist who was interested in studies of the *magnetosphere*.

with fevers and chills and a runny nose. Before the mission was over, all three of the crew had come down with the cold. It made them all short-tempered and cranky.

Apollo 7's three astronauts spent almost 11 full days in space, circling Earth every 90 minutes. They traveled fairly close to Earth, in an oval orbit that took them 183 miles (295 km) from Earth's surface at its highest point.

NASA was happy with the mission's accomplishments and called it a "101 percent successful mission." The achievements of the Apollo 7 mission renewed the nation's confidence in Apollo and the U.S. space program. Project Apollo was spaceborne at last. The triumph had been a long time coming.

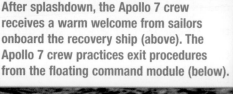

After splashdown, the Apollo 7 crew receives a warm welcome from sailors onboard the recovery ship (above). The Apollo 7 crew practices exit procedures from the floating command module (below).

Straight to the Moon!

When you think of going to the Moon, you probably think of astronauts Neil Armstrong and Buzz Aldrin. As members of the Apollo 11 crew, they landed the *Eagle* at Tranquility Base and took the first steps on the lunar surface. While they were the first astronauts to land on the Moon, they were not the first to travel to the Moon. That honor goes to the astronauts of the Apollo 8 and 10 missions.

Apollo 8 was the first piloted mission launched by the big Saturn V rocket. For the first time in history, human beings traveled beyond Earth orbit to another object in the solar system. Its crew, astronauts Frank Borman, Jim Lovell, and William Anders would also become the first humans to travel behind the Moon.

The news that *Apollo 8* might go to the Moon was not given to the crew until August 1968—just 4 months before the scheduled launch date. Astronaut Deke Slayton, who ran the astronaut office, called Borman, the crew commander, for an emergency meeting. Behind closed doors, he explained that the U.S. Central Intelligence Agency had discovered that the Soviets were planning a lunar flyby before the end of the year. NASA wanted to shift *Apollo 8* from an Earth orbit test to a lunar orbit test to prevent being one-upped. It had happened too often in the past, and now the United States could prevent it from happening again.

Borman agreed to the change, and the crew began training immediately on the simulators. It was a big change and there was no time to spare. When crew member Michael Collins announced that he had to have surgery to remove a painful bone spur, NASA decided to replace him with Jim Lovell.

Each astronaut knew that the risks would be great. There was no margin for error. Every system—from rocket to command module to lunar module—had to work perfectly. The engineers had theories about how the flight plan would work, but that's all they were—theories. They worked well on paper, but nothing about a crewed lunar mission had been proved by practical experience. The Apollo 8 crew would be in for a major challenge.

Apollo 8, ready for liftoff

Finally, launch day arrived. On December 21, 1968, the crew arrived at the launchpad before dawn. The giant Saturn V launcher dominated the scene. The three astronauts stepped into the gantry elevator and ascended to where the CSM was perched. Borman swung into his seat on the left of the capsule, followed by the other two astronauts. They closed the hatch and began running through their checklist, which included more than 400 items.

The Saturn V swayed slightly and fuel gurgled in its innards. The astronauts were sitting on top of 531,000 gallons (2,010,054 Liters) of kerosene and liquid nitrogen that would soon explode into a bundle of awesome energy. The Saturn V was equivalent in power to a small atomic bomb.

The countdown went smoothly, and *Apollo 8* soared skyward under the Saturn V's monstrous power. As soon as the spacecraft reached Earth orbit, the crew began checking all the systems. Everything looked good. They were ready to leave Earth behind and head for the Moon, which took a maneuver called translunar insertion (TLI). Things looked good from Houston, too, and the voice of the capsule communicator (CapCom) came in loud and clear. "All right. You are to go for TLI."

"*Apollo 8*, roger," Borman answered.

The Saturn V's third stage ignited, and *Apollo 8* soon reached a great enough speed to escape Earth's gravity completely. The spacecraft was on its way to the Moon.

Borman triggered the release of the rocket. With a jarring blast, the third stage dropped away. Apollo was on its own.

The crew had divided up their duties. CM pilot Jim Lovell would do the navigating. All three astronauts knew their course had to be plotted precisely, or they would wind up in the wrong part of the Uni-

This view of the Moon was taken from *Apollo 8.*

verse. Bill Anders, who had a keen scientific mind, would monitor the dials and take photos of the Moon. Besides testing the equipment and the flight plan for other missions to the Moon, the Apollo 8 crew would catch the first close-ups of the Moon's surface. Anders knew his photos would be invaluable to the crews who landed there later.

Apollo 8 crossed the Van Allen radiation belts without mishap. As the spacecraft moved farther and farther from Earth, it began to look very small. The astronauts realized that they were crossing a new frontier. No one had ever seen these sights before. Their small spacecraft was like a tiny atom in the vast Universe that lay before them.

Finally, the spacecraft entered lunar orbit. Soon it would be time to pass behind the Moon and within 70 miles (113 km) of the lunar surface. From CapCom came the message, "All systems GO. Safe journey, guys."

"Thanks a lot, troops," Anders answered. "See you on the other side."

The crew burned *Apollo 8*'s engines to slow its pace and put the spacecraft in orbit. The exercise worked perfectly. *Apollo 8* would be on the other side of the Moon for only a brief time, but no communication was possible with Earth for that frightening few minutes.

Finally, after 36 minutes, an announcement came from the little spacecraft so far from home.

"Go ahead, Houston, *Apollo 8*."

They were safe. From the Moon, the astronauts could see no evidence of the civilization they had left behind. However, over the radio, they could faintly hear the cheers from people 240,098 miles (386,400 km) away.

Like the Apollo 7 astronauts, the Apollo 8 crew put on television shows for the audience at home—six of them throughout the flight. Now it was Christmas Eve, and they read from the Bible. It was a moving moment for many Americans and others worldwide—a symbol of humanity, for all its frailty, moving beyond the cradling Earth into the vast Universe. The Apollo 8 television shows were seen in Europe, Japan, all the Americas, and even in Moscow.

After orbiting the Moon ten times, *Apollo 8* headed home. The long voyage went smoothly. As the time for reentry approached, scientists and engineers became nervous. This was the trickiest part of the mission. The Apollo spacecraft would be traveling at a very high speed—

Bill Anders (left), Jim Lovell (center), and Frank Borman (right) pose for photographers in their spacesuits.

about 25,000 miles (40,250 km) per hour—when it reached Earth's atmosphere. The angle of reentry had to be just right to make use of the atmosphere's friction. If the angle was too steep, the atmosphere would crush the spacecraft. If it was too shallow, the spacecraft would be flung back out into space, where the astronauts would be lost forever.

Luckily, everything went according to plan. *Apollo 8* splashed down safely on December 27. For a short while at least, Borman, Lovell, and Anders became the only people on Earth who had ever been to the Moon.

Lunar Ferry Tryout

The Apollo 8 mission proved that NASA had the rocket power to take humans to the Moon, but that was not the crux of John Kennedy's challenge. Landing humans on the Moon was still the goal "before the decade was out," and the little spacecraft that would take crews there had not yet been tested and approved for human descent to the lunar surface.

James McDivitt, David Scott, and Russell Schweickart had the job of making sure the lunar module would work in space. NASA wanted to test the LM close to home, so it was back to Earth orbit for the Apollo 9 crew.*

Apollo 9 lifted off on March 3, 1969. Fellow astronauts called it a "charmed" mission. There was no problem with the panels on the S4B. *Apollo 9* docked easily and picked up the LM. On the fifth day of orbit, Rusty Schweickart and Jim McDivitt floated through the hatch in the CSM (*Gumdrop*) and into the lunar module (*Spider*). They closed the hatch and checked everything over.

Then they pulled the little spacecraft away from *Gumdrop. Spider* was a good name for the little lunar module. It was small, spindly, and awkward looking. Schweickart and McDivitt tried out all its systems—especially the descent and ascent engines. Using *Spider's* own

---

* Originally, McDivitt's crew was supposed to test the lunar module first, and then Frank Borman's crew would refine the tests. *Apollo 10* was supposed to make the first landing on the Moon. When Borman's crew was sent to the Moon without the lunar module, all that changed. By January the new plan was refined. *Apollo 10* would perform a full dress rehearsal and test the lunar module in Moon orbit. If the *Apollo 10* LM tests went poorly, *Apollo 11* would conduct additional tests. But if the tests went well, *Apollo 11* would land on the Moon.

Apollo 9 astronauts David Scott (left), Jim McDivitt (center), and Rusty Schweickart (right) smile for photographers.

rockets, they traveled up to 111 miles (179 km) away from the CSM. Everything worked well. After about 6 hours, the astronauts brought *Spider* back to *Gumdrop*, where Dave Scott was waiting anxiously. The LM edged slowly up to the mother ship, closed in, and slipped into place with a clap. Delighted with their tremendous success, Schweickart

Rusty Schweickart: Energy Expert

Russell "Rusty" Schweickart left NASA in 1969 to become chairman of the California Energy Commission. After the accident that occurred at the Three Mile Island nuclear reactor near Harrisburg, Pennsylvania, on March 28, 1979, Schweickart headed a task force on emergency preparedness in the face of such catastrophes.

and McDivitt floated back through the hatch and took their seats aboard the CSM.

Everything worked so well that it's easy to forget the danger the astronauts were in. If anything had gone wrong, Schweickart and McDivitt could not have landed on Earth. The LM was designed to land on the Moon, where gravity is slight and there is no atmosphere. *Spider* could not have withstood the intense heat created by reentry into Earth's atmosphere. If the two astronauts had not been able to dock back up with *Gumdrop*, it would have been a very bad day in space.

Astronaut David Scott stands in the open hatch of the *Apollo 9* command module, which is docked to the service module. In the background. you can see the lunar module and Earth.

Chapter 4

Dress
Rehearsal

Project Apollo was going well. The Saturn rockets were working
beautifully. A spacecraft had successfully flown to the Moon and
back. The lunar module's engines and docking apparatus all worked
fine—so did its life-support system and its control systems. Reentry in
the command module went smoothly. Everything had been tested, and
finally, the Apollo program was ready for a full dress rehearsal.

Gene Cernan, John Young, and Thomas Stafford took *Apollo 10*
out for this final test, launching on May 18, 1969. The flight was in
every way a dress rehearsal, completing all but the final landing step.
When the spacecraft achieved lunar orbit, Cernan and Stafford went
through the hatch, powered up *Snoopy*, the *Apollo 10* LM, and backed
away from *Charlie Brown*, the CSM. Then they took *Snoopy* for a test

Apollo 10 astronauts Eugene Cernan (left), John Young (center), and Tom Stafford (right) prepare take off for the Moon.

drive. They circled the Moon four times and descended twice to within 50,000 feet (15,240 m) of the Moon's surface.

The astronauts were fascinated by the surface of the Moon. They took a look at the Sea of Tranquility, where *Apollo 11* would land, and reported that it was smooth, with only a few pockmarks and a scattering of shallow craters. Things were looking good.

Meanwhile, Young completed thirty-two revolutions around the Moon, looking down on the strange, bleak surface below him. When Cernan and Stafford were satisfied that they had tested *Snoopy* thoroughly, they *jettisoned* the lunar descent module to free the LM of its weight. (If they had landed, they would have left the descent module on the Moon's surface.) The firing gave them a jolt, but they turned on the power in the ascent engine and boosted Snoopy's altitude to join up with Young and *Charlie Brown*.

At Kennedy Space Center in Cape Canaveral, Florida, the *Apollo 10* lunar module (left) and command service module (right) are prepared for their upcoming flight.

Apollo 10 was the first spaceflight to carry a color television onboard, and the crew made 19 broadcasts during their 8-day mission—a total of 5 hours and 46 minutes that gave everyone a chance to go to the Moon, in a way. Seeing it all in color made a big difference.

In the first of these filmings, Gene Cernan was recorded performing the maneuver that would dock *Charlie Brown* and *Snoopy*. As John Young put *Charlie Brown* through a 180-degree turn, a tiny planet Earth came into view. Americans were suddenly struck by the enormity of what was was happening right before their eyes.

On May 26, *Apollo 10* returned safely to Earth. The mission had been a resounding success. Everything was ready for *Apollo 11*.

"The *Eagle* Has Landed"

Less than 2 months after *Apollo 10* splashed down, *Apollo 11*—the first landing on the Moon—was ready for liftoff. The launch rocket and the spacecraft had traveled less than 1 mile (1.6 km) per hour from Vandenburg Air Force Base to Pad 39-A at Cape Canaveral, Florida. The countdown test at the launchpad ended successfully on July 3, and liftoff was set for July 16, 1969. The mission was carefully timed so that *Eagle, Apollo 11*'s little lunar module, would touch down on the Moon's surface at daybreak.

Astronaut Buzz Aldrin would later recall the hubbub surrounding the launch. "As far as I could see," he said, "there were people and cars lining the beaches and highways. The surf was just beginning to rise out of an azure-blue ocean. I could see the massiveness of the Saturn V rocket . . . " It was a day to remember.

A Crew of Veterans

All three Apollo 11 crew members had flown in the Gemini program, and all three were excellent astronauts. Neil Armstrong was the commander of the mission. He had previously commanded *Gemini 8*, the first mission to dock two spacecraft. He had faced an emergency situation when the two spacecraft began to buck wildly. Armstrong had to undock and gain control of *Gemini 8*, which continued to gyrate because it had a defective thruster. The rest of the mission had to be abandoned. The excellent skills Armstrong showed as commander on that flight made him an excellent choice for the first piloted landing on the Moon.

Apollo 11 astronauts Neil Armstrong (left) and Buzz Aldrin (right) were chosen to become the first two humans to walk on the Moon, while Mike Collins (center) would keep watch as pilot of the command service module (CSM).

Buzz Aldrin had performed the most productive EVA yet in the last Project Gemini mission, *Gemini 12*. He had restored confidence in what, up to then, had been a dicey experience for astronauts. Aldrin logged 2 hours and 9 minutes of continuous work in space. He, too, was a natural choice for this mission because EVA experience would be critical. As the pilot of the lunar module *Eagle*, he would become one of the first two humans to walk on the surface of the Moon.

Michael Collins was a veteran of the Gemini 10 mission, which had involved both rendezvous and docking. He and John Young had also changed orbits during that mission. On the Apollo 11 mission, he would pilot the command module *Columbia*, while Armstrong and Aldrin explored the Moon below.

Apollo 11 lifted off on July 16, 1969. By July 20, the spacecraft had arrived at the Moon. Armstrong and Aldrin moved weightlessly from *Columbia* into *Eagle*. They undocked *Eagle*, pulled away from the CSM, and began descending toward the broad, gray surface below them.

Liftoff! At 9:32 A.M. on July 16, 1969, the *Apollo 11* spacecraft thunders upward from Kennedy Space Center and begins its long voyage to the Moon.

Collins held *Columbia* steady in a circular orbit as his eyes followed the lunar module to the Moon. For him, a lonely watch began.

The voice of CapCom came through loud and clear: "*Eagle*, Houston. If you read, you're a go for powered descent. Over." No answer came.

Collins repeated the message, "*Eagle*, this is *Columbia*. They just gave you a 'go' for powered descent."

The *Eagle* antenna was pointed slightly in the wrong direction, so it had failed to pick up the go-ahead. This was not a good moment to be out of communication. Aldrin and Armstrong noticed and fixed the problem. Then they triggered the ignition. The descent engine started. Armstrong watched the readouts as the computer and radar system coordinated the *attitude* and engine power. Aldrin watched the landmarks and timed them. They were landing long—too far from their planned site.

Suddenly, an error message came from the computer: 1202. Armstrong reported it, without knowing what it meant. This problem had never come up before. The reply came back from Mission Control: The computer was on overload—but really it just meant it was processing. The order came to ignore the warning. It happened three more times—and it was unnerving.

At about 7,500 feet (2,289 m), *Eagle* turned over, its legs sticking out, and Armstrong and Aldrin could see where they were headed. The engine slowed. Now they were about 3,000 feet (915 m) from the lunar surface. Another alarm: 1201. Another overload. Now they were skimming the surface. Armstrong spied a rugged clutter of boulders ahead. At 300 feet (91 m), he veered slightly left with the manual control to miss the boulders. Now a big crater lay ahead. Their altitude was only 60 feet (18 m), and they had only 60 seconds of fuel left. Armstrong maneuvered quickly and brought the spacecraft down gently and landed in a spot with no boulders and no crater walls.

"Houston, Tranquility Base here. The *Eagle* has landed."

"Roger, Tranquility," replied the CapCom. The room at Mission Control broke into wild applause. The ground crew at Houston, and the rest of the world, could breathe again—and so could Neil Armstrong and Buzz Aldrin. It had been tricky, but they made it down. The steady ground below them was the surface of the Moon.

First Step

The two astronauts decided not to take the planned 4-hour rest period aboard *Eagle*. Fatigue and taking a nap were the farthest things from their minds. They began getting ready for their first great adventure. Wearing their white pressurized suits and helmets, they depressurized the cramped interior of the LM. Everything took much longer than they had expected. Finally, they opened the hatch.

With millions of people on Earth watching their televisions, Armstrong backed out of the hatch and carefully ventured down *Eagle*'s 10-foot (3-m) ladder. As he continued to grip the ladder, he stretched his foot from the bottom rung to the surface.

"That's one small step for [a] man, one giant leap for mankind," he exclaimed. He took a sample of the soil immediately, just in case they had to leave suddenly and didn't get another chance. Then he began to look around. He was elated. The first human had arrived on the Moon.

Armstrong did not sink in dust up to his knees, or even up to his ankles, as some people had feared. The life-support system on his back worked well, and the pressurized suit was easy to walk in. The Moon's reduced gravity—one-sixth of Earth's—made getting around easier than in weightlessness or on Earth.

Aldrin descended to the lunar surface, and the two astronauts began to explore. They were careful not to stray more than 200 feet (60 m) from the safety of *Eagle*'s shelter and ascent engine. No one had ever been on the Moon before, and no one knew exactly what to expect. As they bounded about, they looked a little like kangaroos with fishbowl heads.

Astronaut Buzz Aldrin prepares to step onto the surface of the Moon. This photo was taken from the Moon's surface by Neil Armstrong.

It's almost surprising how often the name Jules Verne (1828–1905) turns up when astronauts and rocket builders talk about why they got involved in space. His books and stories have inspired countless scientists, astronauts, and writers. Neil Armstrong, the first human to walk on the Moon, read Verne's stories as a boy, and so did Soviet cosmonaut Yuri Gagarin, the first human in space.

Readers and classic science-fiction film fans still enjoy Verne's *Journey to the Center of the Earth* (1864) and *Twenty Thousand Leagues Under the Sea* (1870). The story that captured the young hearts of the future space community, though, was his amazing novel *From the Earth to the Moon* (1865).

This fast-paced, exciting novel was published more than 100 years before the *Apollo 11* Moon landing. Yet, Verne had his heroes begin their space journey very close to the site of the Apollo launches at Cape Canaveral in Florida. He also correctly gave the initial velocity needed to escape from Earth's gravity.

In the novel's sequel, *Around the Moon* (1870), Verne correctly described the effects of weightlessness in space. He also had his heroes' spacecraft re-enter Earth's atmosphere and splash down in the Pacific Ocean only 3 miles (4.8 km) from the site where *Apollo 11* landed when it returned from the Moon in 1969.

Verne didn't always get everything exactly right, but his novels were filled with many fantastic elements. His imagination and drive to explore the unknown continue to inspire readers today.

Fiction or fact? Note the similarities between this illustration of the "moon projectile" that appeared in Jules Verne's novel *From Earth to the Moon* (left) and the Apollo 11 command module (right).

In this photograph taken from the *Apollo 11* CSM by Mike Collins, Earth shines in the background as Armstrong and Aldrin return from the Moon's surface in the lunar module.

Armstrong and Aldrin did their work. They set out experiments and gathered up rock samples. By the time they were finished, they had 44 pounds (20 kg) of rock to take home. They even dug up a few rocks from about 7 inches (18 cm) below the surface. The samples they collected had an average age of about 4 billion years.

The two astronauts stayed on the moon for 21 hours and 36 minutes. On July 21, they lifted off using *Eagle*'s ascent module. They left the descent portion of the LM behind to reduce the spacecraft's weight. Armstrong and Aldrin docked back up with *Columbia*, which was still orbiting 70 miles (113 km) above the surface. They returned through the hatch to the relative safety of the Columbia cockpit. Then the CSM pulled out of lunar orbit and headed back to Earth.

The 8-day mission came to end on July 24, but Aldrin and Armstrong spent the next 3 weeks in quarantine. No one knew for sure whether they might have picked up alien microorganisms on the faraway world they had just visited. Luckily, no such problem turned up.

Neil Armstrong and Buzz Aldrin were heroes. They were characters in a science fiction story that came true.

To the Ocean of Storms

By late 1969, the Apollo program was ready for its next trip to the Moon. The *Apollo 12* LM touched down 5 days later on the Ocean of Storms. The landing site was about 950 miles (1,500 km) from the Apollo 11 site. They landed less than 100 feet (30 m) from the target. Alan Bean and Pete Conrad spent more than 30 hours on the surface and a total of 15 hours and 32 minutes outside the spacecraft. The

Alan Bean: Space Artist

Alan Bean walked on the Moon during the Apollo 12 mission and spent 59 days orbiting Earth as commander of the second U.S. Skylab flight. Today, his memories of those exciting days are captured on canvas allowing the entire world to share his rare experiences.

Born in Wheeler, Texas, on March 15, 1932, Bean received his Bachelor of Science degree in aeronautical engineering in 1955. He began taking art classes at night while working as a test pilot in 1962. He continued taking art classes "off and on" after that.

"It was just a hobby," he says. But after leaving NASA in 1981, Bean realized, "I might be able to paint some things that no one ever painted—people on the Moon." Displayed in many art galleries, and featured in numerous books, Alan Bean's striking paintings of astronauts in action capture not only what it feels like to be living and working in space, but the indomitable spirit of the space program and humankind's heroic outward quest toward the stars.

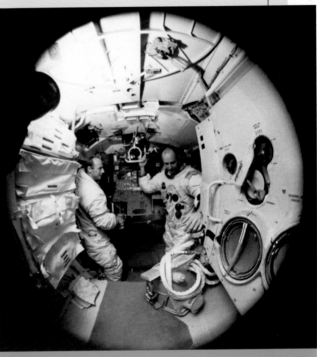

A fish-eye view of Apollo 12 astronauts Pete Conrad (left) and Alan Bean inside a training simulator at the Kennedy Space Center

astronauts took a look at the *Surveyor 3* spacecraft, a robot probe that had landed on the Moon $2\frac{1}{2}$ years earlier. They also took photos of other possible exploration sites.

Chapter 6

Explosion in Space

When *Apollo 13* lifted off on April 11, 1970, there was no reason to expect anything but another smooth mission. However, *Apollo 13* turned out to be the most frightening mission of the Apollo program. About 56 hours into the mission, the bad news came in to Mission Control: "Houston," said astronaut Jim Lovell's voice, "we've had a problem here."

By now, the story is legendary, although the Hollywood version differs slightly from the truth. Liftoff went smoothly—so did the third-stage thrust that set the mission on its path to the Moon and its docking with the lunar module *Aquarius. Apollo 13* was coasting, and had nearly reached the Moon. The CapCom had even remarked that the flight controllers were bored.

On April 11, 1970, *Apollo 13* roared into space.

Suddenly, an explosion in the service module created a critical emergency. Jim Lovell, John Swigert, and Fred Haise were marooned some 200,000 miles (322,000 km) from home. Fuel cells began to fail. The oxygen pressure was falling. Minutes later, the crew lost all oxygen and power in the command and service modules. The command module *Odyssey* was deathly ill.

Landing on the Moon suddenly became the last concern on anyone's mind. Mission Control had to come up with a plan, and quickly, to get the astronauts back home. The flight director told the crew to power up the lunar module. It looked like the astronauts' only hope. Aboard this little lifeboat, the 3-person crew had to live for 4 days on provisions intended to keep 2 men for 2 days.

The crew would need the LM's inertial guidance system for navigating, and it would have to be reconfigured for the new scenario. In addition, the flight path had to be changed so that the spacecraft could get a *gravity assist* as it came from behind the Moon.

The lunar module was cold, and the crew was tired. Would there be enough oxygen to get them back alive? At one point, it became clear that a deadly level of carbon dioxide was building up in the spacecraft. The crew was using both the LM's oxygen supply and its scrubbers— lithium hydroxide canisters that purify the air. But the scrubbers were designed for use by two men, not three. To make things worse, they were malfunctioning. Fortunately, the teams in Mission Control figured out a way to make the command module's lithium hydroxide canisters work inside the lunar module. The crew followed the instructions carefully, and the procedure worked.

To get the crew back earlier and to regain control over the spacecraft, NASA decided that the command module should separate from

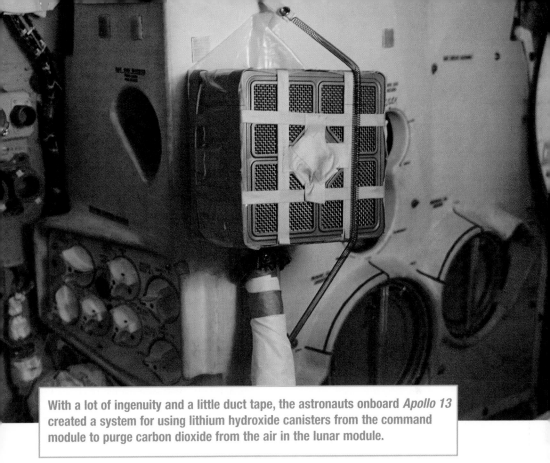

With a lot of ingenuity and a little duct tape, the astronauts onboard *Apollo 13* created a system for using lithium hydroxide canisters from the command module to purge carbon dioxide from the air in the lunar module.

the service module, which was still venting gas. After it was ejected, the crew could see a gaping hole in the service module. "There's one whole side of that spacecraft missing!" Lovell exclaimed.

The astronauts were nearing Earth. Reentry would be tricky. They would have to crawl back into *Odyssey* because the LM was not designed for descending into Earth's atmosphere. The crew powered *Odyssey* back up and separated from their trusty lifeboat. "Farewell, *Aquarius*, and we thank you," Lovell said with a typical sense of the moment.

Now, as long as everything went right with reentry, *Apollo 13* and its crew would be home free, but more tension lay ahead. Mission Control always lost communications for about the first 3 minutes of reentry. This time the dead air lasted longer. Tension mounted. Then

Following their perilous mission, *Apollo 13* astronauts Fred Haise (left), John Swigert (center), and Jim Lovell (right) are welcomed home by Rear Admiral Donald C. Davis.

tracking data picked up a signal—the *Odyssey* had survived, but were the crew members OK?

Finally, the ground controllers received a response. Everyone was OK. Probably few people have ever been as glad to see the familiar outlines of Earth again as Jim Lovell, John Swigert, and Fred Haise were at the end of the Apollo 13 mission.

After splashdown, Project Apollo went on hold until the problems with *Apollo 13* could be studied. NASA formed an investigation board, and the results came back quickly. The explosion was caused by a combination of human error—an exposed wire in the service module—and a design flaw. The problems were fixed before the next mission flew.

Chapter 7

Roaming and Roving the Moon

Apollo 14 carried Alan Shepard, the first U.S. astronaut to enter space, back to space for the first time since 1961. A prolonged inner-ear infection, bad news for any pilot, had kept him from even flying solo in Earth's atmosphere. The astronaut was grounded in mid-career. Now, with the help of surgery, Shepard's ear had healed in time for him to make a triumphant return to space.

Golfing on the Moon

Alan Shepard had been in space before—but that ride had been a lot different from the one he was about to take. The first U.S. astronaut had entered space in a tiny one-person Mercury capsule atop a little

Astronaut Alan Shepard prepares for his Apollo 14 mission.

Redstone rocket for a relatively small hop of 116 miles (187 km). The whole trip from liftoff to splashdown had taken only 15 minutes. Now, after 10 years away from rockets and spacecraft, he was commander of a mission to the Moon—the most complex mission anyone could fly.

Some of the other astronauts were a little angry—especially those who were hoping for an assignment to go to the Moon. Everyone knew Alan Shepard was a top astronaut. He was good, but how could he be that good? Let him wait in line. However, Shepard had a lot of clout with fellow Mercury Seven astronaut Deke Slayton, who made the decisions about who flew what and when. Shepard wanted to return to space, and like nearly all the other astronauts, he wanted to walk on the Moon.

Apollo 14 was Shepard's mission. He had trained hard. At 47, he was in top physical condition. His crew, Stuart Roosa and Edgar Mitchell, were ready too, but was their Apollo spacecraft?

When the CM, *Kitty Hawk*, refused to hook up with the LM, *Antares*, the Apollo 14 mission threatened to end early. Without a lunar module, there could be no landing. Stuart Roosa finally gave up coddling the mechanism and just rammed the little lander. The docking adapter clicked in and pulled *Antares* away from the SB4. *Apollo 14* was on its way. The rest of the journey to the Moon was uneventful, but when it came to taking *Antares* down to the surface, a problem

Ed Mitchell (left), Stu Roosa (center), and Alan Shepard (right) learn to operate Apollo's controls.

with the radar turned up. Despite this difficulty, Shepard flew *Antares* to the surface and landed smoothly in the region of Fra Mauro. As he stepped onto the surface, he said, "It's been a long way, but we're here."

Geologists think that about 5 million years ago, a *meteorite* struck the Fra Mauro region of the Moon, scooping out a valley about half the length of the West Coast of the United States. Shepard and Edgar Mitchell took a little two-wheeled cart out on their expeditions and gathered up material that provides clues about the formation of the solar system.

The EVAs went well, and just as the astronauts were getting ready to leave, Shepard surprised everyone by taking out a couple of golf balls and a golf club fashioned from one of the rock tools in the cart. An avid golfer, he thought he'd show Americans what some real golfing looked like. He whacked at the balls a couple of times. He missed one, but sent the other sailing, as he said, "for miles and miles"—well, anyway at least six times farther than it would have gone on Earth. It was a good demonstration of the Moon's weak gravity.

Alan Shepard: Moon Golfer

Alan Shepard served as chief of the astronaut office from 1963 to 1969 and from 1971 to 1974. In 1974 he resigned from NASA and the Navy, where he had achieved the rank of rear admiral. In 1979, he received the Medal of Honor for his spaceflights.

In addition to his duties at NASA, Shepard avidly pursued private enterprise. He served on the board of directors of several successful companies and started his own firm. He had become a millionaire even before he retired from NASA. After retirement, he devoted all his energies to investment and business interests, such as banking, oil wells, real estate, and quarter horses. For several years he also headed the Mercury Seven Foundation (now the Astronaut Scholarship Foundation), which raises funds for science and engineering scholarships.

Alan Shepard died of leukemia on July 22, 1998. He was 74.

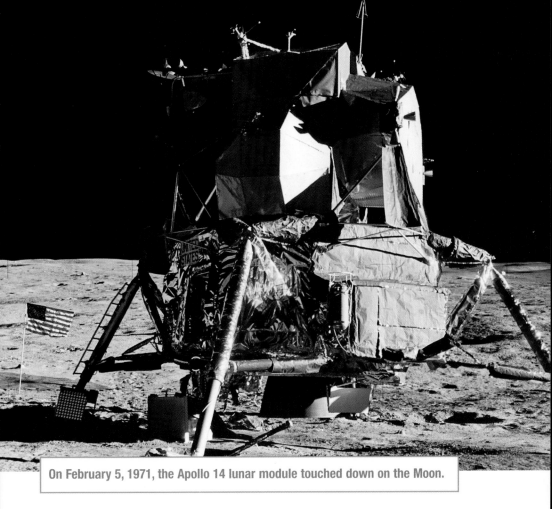

On February 5, 1971, the Apollo 14 lunar module touched down on the Moon.

Shepard and Mitchell packed up the Moon rocks they had collected during their 33 hours and 30 minutes on the lunar surface. They headed back to *Antares* and ascended to rejoin Roosa on the orbiting CSM. Then the crew headed back to Earth.

Riding the Rover

The *Apollo 12* and *Apollo 14* astronauts walked on the Moon as Armstrong and Aldrin had done, but the astronauts who traveled on the last three Apollo missions used a lunar roving vehicle to help them get

The *Apollo 15* crew was the first to drive the lunar roving vehicle across the Moon's surface.

around. The lunar rover could roll across the flat, hardened areas of volcanic rock and ash or clamber around craters.

The astronauts on the Apollo 15, 16, and 17 missions brought back samples of Moon rock, took photographs, examined landforms, and spent as much time as they could driving the rover across the Moon's dusty terrain. The rover worked so well on the Moon that astronauts naturally began thinking of other surfaces it might do well on—for instance, the surface of Mars.

En route to the Moon, the lunar rover was strapped to the outside of the lunar module, "like a piano tied to a moving van," as Gene Cernan put it in his book *The Last Man on the Moon.* Once the LM landed, the astronauts unloaded the rover and unfolded it like a sofa bed. Its chassis was about 10 feet (3 m) long and 4 feet (1.2 m) high.

On Earth, it weighed 460 pounds (209 kg), but on the Moon, it weighed only 76 pounds (34.5 kg).

With its wire-mesh wheels, the rover would never get a flat tire, but the astronauts still had to plan their outings carefully. No repair service would answer calls for help. So they had to be careful not to drive the rover any farther than they could walk back, using the oxygen they had with them. The rover could go up to 8 miles (13 km) per hour, running on batteries. It was fitted with a television camera, a computer, and a gyroscope for navigating. It was perfect for transporting rock samples and reducing fatigue.

Got Wheels!

Apollo 15 was the first mission to use the new lunar rover. The Apollo 15 astronauts hoped to find some clues to the origin of the Moon in the area chosen for their landing, the Hadley Apennine Mountains.

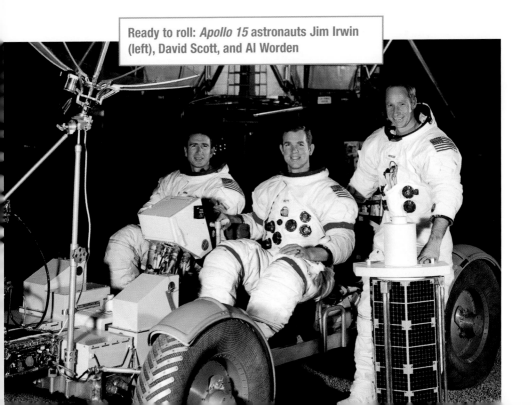

Ready to roll: *Apollo 15* astronauts Jim Irwin (left), David Scott, and Al Worden

This site seemed like a good choice geologically, but the mountainous terrain made landing a challenge. The LM had to set down almost completely vertically to reach the planned landing site. The spot was also dusty so, as the lander lowered toward the surface, the descent engine kicked up such a cloud of dust that the astronauts couldn't see where they were going. They hit hard and skittered a short distance, but they had set down on the plain at Hadley.

Dave Scott and Jim Irwin spent 3 days on the surface. As they took the lunar rover across the surface to the sites of interest, mission scientist Joe Allen could direct the rover's camera by remote control from Earth. The two astronauts found several formations and rocks that looked promising, including one the astronauts named "the Genesis rock." Excited, they wrapped it separately to take back for examination by scientists. They hoped it would contain clues about the Moon's formation.

"The Genesis Rock" was collected by David Scott and Jim Irwin

Meanwhile, orbiting above in *Endeavor*, Al Worden spotted an area on the Moon's surface that was unusual and very dark. He knew the scientists would be interested in this terrain and he began taking pictures. The site, a place named Taurus-Littrow Valley, was later chosen for the *Apollo 17* LM landing.

During this mission, Dave Scott ran a classic experiment to prove a theory first suggested by the sixteenth-century Italian scientist Galileo Galilei. Scott held a feather and a hammer equal distances from the Moon's surface and dropped them both at the same time. According to Galileo, they should both reach the surface at once, regardless of their mass. The test works better in a vacuum than in Earth's atmosphere. Since the Moon's surface comes close to vacuum conditions, Scott decided to give the experiment a try. It turns out that Galileo was right.

Scott and Irwin left behind a small figurine of a fallen astronaut and a plaque commemorating the U.S. astronauts and Soviet cosmonauts who had given their lives for space exploration.

The Highlands Await

The next mission didn't launch for nearly 9 months. Originally scheduled for March, the launch date slid into April when Charlie Duke, the LM pilot, came down with pneumonia. When *Apollo 16* finally

Ken Mattingly (left), John Young (center), and Charles Duke (right) faced many challenges during their Apollo 16 mission.

entered space on April 16, 1972, the astronauts faced several challenges. The problems reminded everyone that nothing on the frontier of space is routine.

First, John Young, Ken Mattingly, and Charlie Duke had to solve a problem with leaks in the S4B rocket before they could enter the translunar insertion that started them on their long journey to the Moon. As the astronauts watched the *Orion* lunar module from a window, they noticed some white flaking on its exterior. The flaking turned out to be just some cold and brittle white paint, but once in lunar orbit, the crew discovered a problem with *Orion*'s regulator. They worked out a solution, but then a problem arose with the LM's automatic antenna. The astronauts decided to operate it manually and were soon on their way to their landing site. Then the crew encountered a problem that forced them to put their descent on hold.

Mattingly, who was by now flying the *Casper* command module alone, was having trouble with a propulsion system. It was causing oscillations, or unusual shuddering. Under these conditions, Young and Duke could not be allowed to land. Six hours went by as Mission Control tried to determine how serious the problem was. After two full orbits around the Moon, NASA's decision came through: landing was a go. However, *Orion* would now have to be repositioned. New data was sent from Houston, and *Orion* descended to the surface.

Once on the Moon, the two astronauts were so exhausted that they immediately went to sleep on *Orion*'s floor. The next morning, they climbed down the ladder and began the first of their three expeditions using the lunar rover. In all, they covered some 17 miles (27 km) as they explored craters, examined huge boulders, and collected 215 pounds (97 kg) of rocks. Overall, their surface experiments and EVAs

John Young trains for an EVA during which he will place a special ultraviolet camera on the Moon's surface.

went well. They also tested a new ultraviolet (UV) camera and spectrometer. The mission remained in lunar orbit 126 hours and completed 64 orbits.

The Last Voyage

During the Apollo program, the scientific community pointed out that a scientist could learn a great deal by traveling to the Moon. The Apollo astronauts had received some training in geology, but they could not examine the surface of the Moon as well as a trained geologist.

For the astronauts, though, giving up one seat in a three-person command module meant having one crew member who wasn't a professional astronaut. Yes, the geologist could interpret the record of rocks better, but an astronaut could fly better, and a mission to the Moon needed a qualified crew whose members could make sound decisions quickly.

Finally, a compromise was made. NASA would send one scientist on the last mission to the Moon. He would train with the other crew members, and he would have to become a licensed airplane pilot. The man chosen for the job was Harrison "Jack" Schmitt.

As *Apollo 17* sat on the launchpad for an afternoon launch, the countdown proceeded on schedule. Then, only moments before liftoff, everything suddenly stopped. Engineers worked frantically to fix a computer glitch. Finally, a few minutes after midnight, the big behemoth known as Saturn V rose through a cloud of mist and headed for the Moon. *Apollo 17* was on its way. Excitement inside the cockpit was intense. Ron Evans let out a huge "Whoopee!" Jack Schmitt—a usually quiet, seriously academic product of Harvard University—lost his reserve and exclaimed, "We're going up! Man, oh man!"

The astronauts made up their lost time during the coast toward the Moon. The command module *Challenger* and the lunar module *America* arrived in lunar orbit on time, and everything went smoothly. *America* set down close to its target in the crater-filled Valley of Taurus-Littrow.

Eugene Cernan and Jack Schmitt spent 78 hours guiding the lunar rover nearly 22 miles (35 km). They ventured as far as 4.5 miles (7.3 km) from their base. Their explorations were productive. They took more than 2,000 photographs. They also filled the rover with soil and rock samples weighing a total of 243 pounds (110 kg).

On the first day, Schmitt took time to describe the terrain to scientists in Houston, giving them both a large-scale and more detailed overview of the locale in language that would help geologists understand more about the Moon, its composition, and its origins. It was the first time a geologist had ever been able to see these sights firsthand. Schmitt was delighted with his surroundings. He could easily differentiate among the kinds of rock—they were not hidden beneath a deep layer of fine dust as he had expected.

Cernan and Schmitt left behind explosive materials that would be set off later, after they left to measure seismic profiles on the Moon's

Astronaut Gene Cernan took this photo of astronaut-geologist Harrison Schmitt on the surface of the Moon during the Apollo 17 mission.

surface. They also measured gravity and electrical properties in different areas of the surface. They took a deep core sample and drilled two 8.3-foot (2.5-m) holes in the surface. The holes would be used for heat-flow sensors. The two astronauts did a lot of hard work.

On their second excursion, Cernan and Schmitt were looking around a crater called "Shorty," when Schmitt exclaimed, "Oh, hey—wait a minute— . . . There is orange soil!" Cernan confirmed his description with a wry, "He's not going out of his mind. It really is." On Earth, orange soil would likely mean that oxidized iron was present, and so Schmitt suspected volcanic activity in the area. The find was unique in Moon exploration so far, and Schmitt was excited.

To document the find, the pair dug a trench, took a core sample and scoop samples, and took lots of photographs. They were near the limit of their "walk-back capability," the rule of thumb that instructed them to go no farther and spend no more time than it would take for them to walk back on the oxygen supply they had. Finally they hopped back in the rover and headed back, with Schmitt excitedly discussing the orange soil.

After their third EVA, Cernan revealed a plaque attached to one leg of *Challenger*'s descent module. It said: "Here man completed his first explorations of the Moon December 1972, A.D. May the spirit of peace in which we came be reflected in the lives of all mankind." It was signed by Cernan, Evans, Schmitt, and Richard Nixon, president of the United States.

In a formal statement, Cernan spoke these words: "This is our commemoration that will be here until someone like us, until some of you who are out there, who are the promise of the future, come back to read it again and to further the exploration and the meaning of Apollo."

After parking the rover where the television camera could have a good view of their liftoff, Cernan added, "I believe history will record that America's challenge of today has forged man's destiny of tomorrow." Finally, they packed their samples in *Challenger*'s ascent module, discarded unneeded tools, and lifted off.

On television screens at home, the camera followed the liftoff until Challenger was no longer in sight. Then it panned across the silent and deserted surface of the Moon. When the Apollo capsule splashed down, Television cameras on Earth were ready to capture the action.

Following splashdown (left), *Apollo 17* astronauts Gene Cernan (waving), Harrison Schmitt (right), and Ron Evans (in back) arrived safely aboard the U.S.S. *Tigonderoga* (right).

Last Footprints

Six pairs of Apollo astronauts brought back samples of Moon rock, took photographs, examined landforms, and spent as much time as they could exploring the Moon's dusty terrain. They helped scientists learn a great deal about Earth's desolate, lifeless neighbor—about what it's made of, how it formed, and what has happened to it throughout time. In the process they added a vast store of information to human understanding of the Universe we live in.

The footprints these human beings left remain there today in the airless, breezeless environment of the Moon. They will be there for thousands of years—as long as no one disturbs them and no object collides with the Moon. They are symbols of the human desire to know and to understand. They are a record of the incredible achievement represented by six Moon landings.

Chapter 8

Ending an Era

The Apollo spacecraft did more than carry the first humans to the Moon. After *Apollo 17* landed, spare parts were used for two other projects. Apollo's first legacy, known as *Skylab*, was a space station designed for scientific observations and experiments. *Skylab* used surplus Apollo hardware—Saturn booster rockets, command modules, and service modules. The plan was economical, efficient, and productive, as well as adventurous.

NASA converted an empty, unused booster rocket and used it to build the spacecraft's main segment, called the workshop. It had two levels, with separate compartments for living and working. This segment was assembled and outfitted on Earth and lifted into orbit by a spare Saturn V rocket.

This photo of the Skylab space station orbiting
Earth was taken on February 8, 1974.

The Soviets had built space stations, but no one had ever before
put a space station this large into orbit. It had the volume of a three-
bedroom house, and on Earth it weighed nearly 6,000 pounds
(2,721.6 kg).

Between May 1973 and January 1974, three crews of astronauts
lived and worked aboard *Skylab*. They studied the Sun and Earth
resources, and, in the process, took a wealth of photos. They also performed many EVAs. They even examined the effects of weightlessness
on themselves and other living things, including a pair of spiders.

These studies provided new information about the solar system, our planet, and working in zero gravity.

Originally, NASA had planned to keep *Skylab* in orbit by nudging it with its next planned launch program, the Space Shuttle. However, other factors intervened. First, Space Shuttle plans were delayed. Then the United States became deeply involved in the Vietnam War. With so much government energy and funding going to the war, space exploration became a low priority.

Astronaut Pete Conrad trains for his mission aboard *Skylab*.

Because *Skylab* could not maintain its orbit without a nudge and NASA had no way of saving it, the space station plummeted to Earth on July 11, 1979. It broke up during reentry, and pieces landed in the Pacific Ocean and in uninhabited regions of Australia.

ASTP: Handshake in the Sky

In 1975, in a rare Cold War gesture of peace and cooperation between the Soviet Union and the United States, the two countries completed a joint mission. Known officially as the Apollo-Soyuz Test Project (ASTP), or simply Apollo-Soyuz, the mission signaled the beginning of a thaw in the Cold War.

Deke Slayton, the only one of the Mercury Seven who had never flown in space, commanded the mission for the United States, American astronauts Thomas Stafford and Vance Brand were also crew members. On the Soviet side, Alexei Leonov also made the trip. In 1965, Leonov had performed the world's first EVA aboard *Voskhod 2*. Fellow cosmonaut Valery Kubasov completed the crew.

On July 15, 1975, after 4 years of preparation, *Apollo 18* and *Soyuz 19* lifted off, each in a different part of the world. *Soyuz 19* launched from Tyuratem in Kazakhstan at 8:20 A.M. eastern daylight time (EDT). *Apollo 18* took off from Kennedy Space Center in Florida at 3:50 P.M. EDT. As soon as the Apollo spacecraft reached Earth orbit, it began pursuing the Soyuz craft. When Apollo caught up, it rendezvoused and docked using a special docking adapter that had been installed to make the two spacecraft compatible. The two crews crowded into the Apollo spacecraft to shake hands in an internationally televised gesture.

Alexei Leonov: Space Artist

Shortly after the Soviet and American space capsules rendezvoused during the Apollo-Soyuz Test Project, Soviet cosmonaut Alexei Leonov shook hands in space with U.S. astronaut Thomas Stafford. The moment was certainly historic—both in the annals of space and in the relations between the two superpowers.

Leonov, though, had made history before. As the second pilot aboard the Soviet spacecraft *Voskhod 2*, launched on March 18, 1965, he ventured into space in the first space walk. He spent 24 minutes alone outside his spacecraft.

Leonov was born in Russia in 1934 and trained as a fighter pilot. While spending 2 years as a fighter pilot in various Soviet Air Force units, he also became a skilled parachutist and a military instructor in parachute training.

Because of his daring, intelligence, and skill, he was picked as one of the first twelve Soviet cosmonauts in 1960. After the Apollo-Soyuz mission, he was placed in command of the Soviet cosmonaut team.

Leonov is also a talented writer and artist. He has written ten books about space and published three art books. His paintings—based on his experiences and observations in space—have appeared in exhibitions around the world and on Soviet stamps.

Cosmonaut Alexei Leonov (standing on right) is shown here with other members of the Apollo-Soyuz Test Project crew.

An artist's conception of the *Apollo 18* CSM docking with *Soyuz 19*

By July 21, the Soviet cosmonauts had returned home safely. They were exhausted, but the mission had gone well, and the astronauts and cosmonauts enjoyed getting together and exchanging stories about what they do. The Apollo-Soyuz mission took place 16 years before the Soviet Union dissolved, but it seemed to signal a general warming of the political climate between the two countries.

The Apollo astronauts were still in space, though. They conducted a few experiments and held a press conference from space. On July 24, they

performed what appeared to be a normal reentry and splashdown. However, what television audiences didn't realize was that a near-deadly mistake had occurred, causing an extremely poisonous gas to be expelled into the cockpit. By the time the Apollo CM landed, the astronauts were struggling to remain conscious.

As Slayton tried to get to the oxygen masks, he was thrown into the docking tunnel by the pitching spacecraft. He struggled again to get the masks, and finally managed to get one on. He handed one to Stafford and put one on Brand, who had lost consciousness. All three astronauts survived the emergency, thanks to Slayton's quick thinking. It was a close call.

The Apollo-Soyuz mission brought an end to Project Apollo. It also marked the end of an era. The space race was over, and the United States was victorious. NASA had succeeded in sending many astronauts to the Moon and all had returned safely to Earth. The United States had shown the world that its scientists, engineers, and astronauts had "the right stuff."

With these important goals accomplished, Americans became less interested in space exploration. No more U.S. astronauts entered space until the first piloted Space Shuttle flight in 1981, and no more missions were sent to the Moon until the late 1990s.

The U.S. Space Shuttle opened a new era in space exploration.

Today, public interest in space travel is on the rise again. Crews have begun to live aboard the *International Space Station*. It may not be long before we launch a new initiative to send people to Mars. All this began with the brave astronauts who dared to take the first steps into space.

Apollo Mission Facts

Vital Statistics

Mission	Date of Launch	Astronauts	Highlights
APOLLO 7	October 11, 1968	Wally Schirra, Donn Eisele, Walter Cunningham	First crew to fly the Apollo spacecraft; test in Earth orbit
APOLLO 8	December 21, 1968	Frank Borman, James Lovell, William Anders	First crewed flight around the Moon; launched by the Saturn V rocket
APOLLO 9	March 3, 1969	James McDivitt, David Scott, Russell Schweickart	First test of the LM in Earth orbit; McDivitt and Schweickart take the LM out for a flight and then re-dock with the CM
APOLLO 10	May 18, 1969	Thomas Stafford, John Young, Eugene Cernan	Final test drive before landing on the Moon. Stafford and Cernan take the LM into orbit around the Moon
APOLLO 11	July 16, 1969	Neil Armstrong, Michael Collins, Edwin "Buzz" Aldrin	Armstrong and Aldrin land on the Moon; they spend nearly 2 days on the surface and bring back 44 pounds (20 kg) of lunar material

Mission	Date of Launch	Astronauts	Highlights
Apollo 12	November 14, 1969	Charles "Pete" Conrad, Richard Gordon, Alan Bean	In two EVA walks, Conrad and Bean spend 15 hours and 32 minutes exploring the Moon's surface and collecting samples
Apollo 13	April 11, 1970	James Lovell, John Swigert, Fred Haise	Because of a problem with the spacecraft's SM, Apollo 13 astronauts do not land on the Moon; instead they fly around the Moon and back home to Earth
Apollo 14	January 31, 1971	Alan Shepard, Stuart Roosa, Edgar Mitchell	Astronauts collect samples from the crater Fra Mauro; Shepard plays golf on the Moon's surface
Apollo 15	July 26, 1971	David Scott, Alfred Worden, James Irwin	First mission to use the lunar rover
Apollo 16	April 16, 1972	John Young, Thomas "Ken" Mattingly, Charles Duke	Astronauts conduct observations and experiments on the Moon's surface
Apollo 17	December 7, 1972	Eugene Cernan, Ron Evans, Harrison Schmitt	Civilian geologist Schmitt directs scientific activities during lunar EVAs

Project Apollo: A Timeline

1957 — *Sputnik 1*, the first artificial satellite, is launched by the former Soviet Union.

1958 — *Explorer 1*, the first U.S. satellite, is launched.

1959 — *Pioneer 4* is sent to the Moon to collect information.

1961 — The first piloted Mercury flight carries Alan Shepard into space aboard *Freedom 7*.

1962 — John Glenn becomes the first U.S. astronaut to orbit Earth aboard *Friendship 7*.

1965 — Aboard *Gemini 4*, Ed White performs first space walk by U.S. astronaut.

1966 — *Gemini 8* and unpiloted Agena spacecraft perform the first successful docking exercise in space.

1967 — All three *Apollo 1* astronauts die when the command module bursts into flame during a ground test.

1968 — *Apollo 7* is launched into Earth orbit. It is the first crewed mission using the Apollo spacecraft.

Aboard *Apollo 8*, three U.S. astronauts become the first humans to circle the Moon.

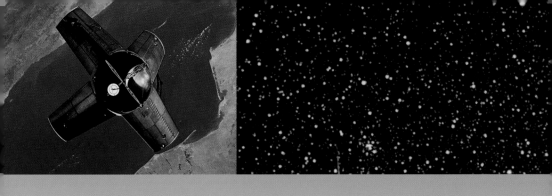

1969 — *Apollo 9* tests the lunar module in Earth orbit.

Apollo 10 acts as a dress rehearsal for a real Moon landing. It goes to the Moon, and astronauts take the lunar module into Moon orbit, but it does not land.

Aboard *Apollo 11*, astronauts Neil Armstrong and Buzz Aldrin become the first human beings to walk on the Moon. More than 1 billion people worldwide watch the event live on television.

Astronauts onboard *Apollo 12* explore the surface of the Moon and collect rock samples.

1970 — Technical problems force three astronauts aboard *Apollo 13* to circle the Moon instead of landing; they return to Earth on reduced power.

The Soviet Union's *Lunokhod 1* rover becomes the first uncrewed moving vehicle on the Moon's surface.

1971 — Astronauts onboard *Apollo 14* collect rock samples. Alan Shepard plays golf. *Apollo 15* astronauts drive NASA's lunar rover on the Moon's surface for the first time.

1972   *Apollo 16* astronauts conduct experiments on the Moon's surface.

Apollo 17, last of the Apollo missions, transports the first civilian to the Moon. Geologist Harrison Schmitt examines and describes the Moon from a geologist's point of view.

attitude—the position of a spacecraft in flight in relation to a fixed reference such as the horizon or another vehicle; also, a spacecraft's orientation with respect to the direction in which it is moving

booster—an extra rocket (sometimes called a *booster rocket*) used to give an additional boost, or lift, to the main cargo and rocket; as their fuel is used up, booster rockets are discarded and fall back to Earth. Some empty booster rockets can be collected and reused.

command module (CM)—the main Apollo spacecraft module; it is the only part of the spacecraft that returns to Earth at the end of a mission

dock—to join physically with another spacecraft, like a ship coming into a dock to tie up. Once docked, astronauts may be able to move from one spacecraft to another.

docking adapter—device that makes docking possible between two spacecraft

extravehicular activity (EVA)—space walk; activity outside a spacecraft

gantry—the huge vertical structure used for servicing a rocket or accessing a spacecraft mounted on a rocket. It is pulled away before liftoff.

gravity assist—a maneuver in which a spacecraft circles a body in space and uses the object's gravitational pull to increase its acceleration

jettison—to cast off or discard

launch vehicle—a rocket or group of rockets that launch an artificial satellite or spacecraft into space

liquid fuel—a fuel, such as gasoline, that exists naturally in a liquid state

lunar module (LM)—portion of the three-part Apollo spacecraft that was used to land on the Moon (the other two are the command and service modules)

magnetosphere—the vast area surrounding Earth that is filled with electrically charged particles and electromagnetic radiation

meteorite—a chunk of dust or rock from space that strikes the surface of another object, such as a moon or planet

multistage rocket—a rocket system that makes use of one or more booster rockets to provide additional lift

orbit—the path an object follows as it revolves around another body in space

payload—how much a rocket can carry

rendezvous—(verb) to meet, to be in the same area at the same time; (noun) a meeting or encounter

satellite—a natural or human-made "moon" that orbits another object, such as a planet or an asteroid. *Sputnik 1* was called an artificial satellite because it was a humanmade object that orbited Earth.

service module (SM)—portion of the Apollo spacecraft that carried fuel, supplies, and engines

thrust—forward push caused in reaction to a high-speed flow of fluid or gases in the opposite direction from a rocket engine

The news from space changes fast, so it's always a good idea to check the copyright date on books, CD-ROMs, and video tapes to make sure that you are getting up-to-date information. One good place to look for current information from NASA is U.S. government depository libraries. There are several in each state.

Bean, Alan, with Andrew Chaiken. *Apollo: An Eyewitness Account by Astronaut/Explorer/Artist/Moonwalker Alan Bean, with an introduction by John Glenn.* Shelton, CT: Greenwich Workshop Press, 1998.

Burrows, William. *This New Ocean: A History of the First Space Age.* New York: Random House, 1998.

Campbell, Ann Jeanette. *The New York Public Library Amazing Space: A Book of Answers for Kids.* New York: John Wiley & Sons, 1997.

Cernan, Eugene, with Don Davis. *The Last Man on the Moon.* New York: St. Martin's Press, 1999.

Chaiken, Andrew. *A Man on the Moon: The Voyages of the Apollo Astronauts.* New York: Viking, 1994.

Lovell, Jim, with Jeffrey Kluger. *Apollo 13.* New York: Pocket Books, 1996.

Schefter, James. *The Race: The Uncensored Story of How America Beat Russia to the Moon.* New York: Doubleday, 1999.

Schirra, Wally, with Richard N. Billings. *Schirra's Space*. Annapolis, MD: Naval Institute Press, 1995.

Slayton, Donald K., with Michael Cassutt. *Deke! U.S. Manned Space: From Mercury to the Shuttle*. New York: St. Martin's Press, 1994.

Spangenburg, Ray, and Diane Moser. *Space People from A to Z*. New York: Facts On File, Inc., 1990.

CD-ROMs

Space: A Visual History of Manned Space Flight, Second Edition
Sumeria, Inc.
100 Eucalyptus Drive
San Francisco, CA 94132

NASA Museum: A Tour Through America's Continuing Exploration of Space
Saturn Five
6380 S. Eastern Ave., Suite 12
Las Vegas, NV 89120

Video Tapes

Apollo 13, directed by Ron Howard, starring Tom Hanks.

History of Spaceflight: Reaching for the Stars. Finley-Holiday Film Corp., 1995.

Out of This World: The Apollo Moon Landings. Finley-Holiday Film Corp., 1988.

Organizations and Online Sites

Many of the sites listed below are NASA sites, with links to many other interesting sources of information about space travel. You can also sign up to receive NASA news on many subjects via e-mail.

Astronomical Society of the Pacific
390 Ashton Avenue
San Francisco, CA 94112

Kennedy Space Center
http://www.ksc.nasa.gov/ksc.html
This site features an overview of shuttle flights as well as information about the Mercury, Gemini, and Apollo programs.

NASA Ask a Space Scientist
NASA scientists answer your questions about astronomy, space, and space missions. The site also has archives and fact sheets.

NASA History
http://history.nasa.gov
This in-depth site has information about all aspects of NASA history.

NASA Human Spaceflight
http://spaceflight.nasa.gov
This is the Internet hub for exploring everything related to human spaceflight, including current stories and realtime data as they break. You can explore the International Space Station, track Space Shuttle flights, trace space history, and see many interesting images.

NASA Newsroom
This site has NASA's latest press releases, status reports, and fact sheets. It includes a NASA News Archive for past reports and a search button for the NASA Web. You can even sign up for e-mail versions of all NASA press releases.

National Space Society
600 Pennsylvania Avenue, S.E., Suite 201
Washington, DC 20003

The Planetary Society
65 North Catalina Avenue
Pasadena, CA 91106-2301

Places to Visit

Check the Internet (*www.skypub.com* is a good place to start), your local visitor's center, or phone directory for planetariums and science museums near you. Here are a few suggestions:

Exploratorium
3601 Lyon Street
San Francisco, CA 94123
Internationally acclaimed interactive science exhibits, including space- and physics-related subjects.

NASA Goddard Space Flight Center
Code 130, Public Affairs Office
Greenbelt, MD 20771
Visitors can see a Moon rock brought back to Earth by Apollo astronauts, as well as other related exhibits.

Space Center Houston
Space Center Houston Information
1601 NASA Road 1
Houston, Texas 77058
Offers a tour and exhibits related to humans in space, including the Apollo missions to the Moon.

Spaceport USA
Kennedy Space Center
Titusville, FL 32899
http://www.ksc.nasa.gov/ksc.html
Museum and special exhibits on the history of space exploration

U.S. Space and Rocket Center
P.O. Box 070015
Huntsville, AL 35807-7015
http://ussrc.com
Exhibits of meteorites and rockets, Spacedome IMAX Theater, full-scale mock-up of the Russian Mir space station, and home of the U.S. Space Camp, where participants learn by doing about space exploration and space science.

Index

Bold numbers indicate illustrations.

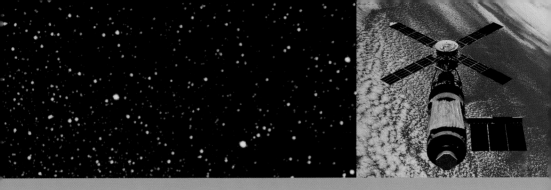

Ray Spangenburg and **Kit Moser** are a husband-and-wife writing team specializing in science and technology. They have written 33 books and more than 100 articles, including a 5-book series on the history of science and a 4-book series on the history of space exploration. As journalists, they covered NASA and related science activities for many years. They have flown on NASA's Kuiper Airborne Observatory, covered stories at the Deep Space Network in the Mojave Desert, and experienced zero gravity on experimental NASA flights out of NASA Ames Research Center. They live in Carmichael, California, with their two dogs, Mencken (a Sharpei mix) and F. Scott Fitz (a Boston Terrier).

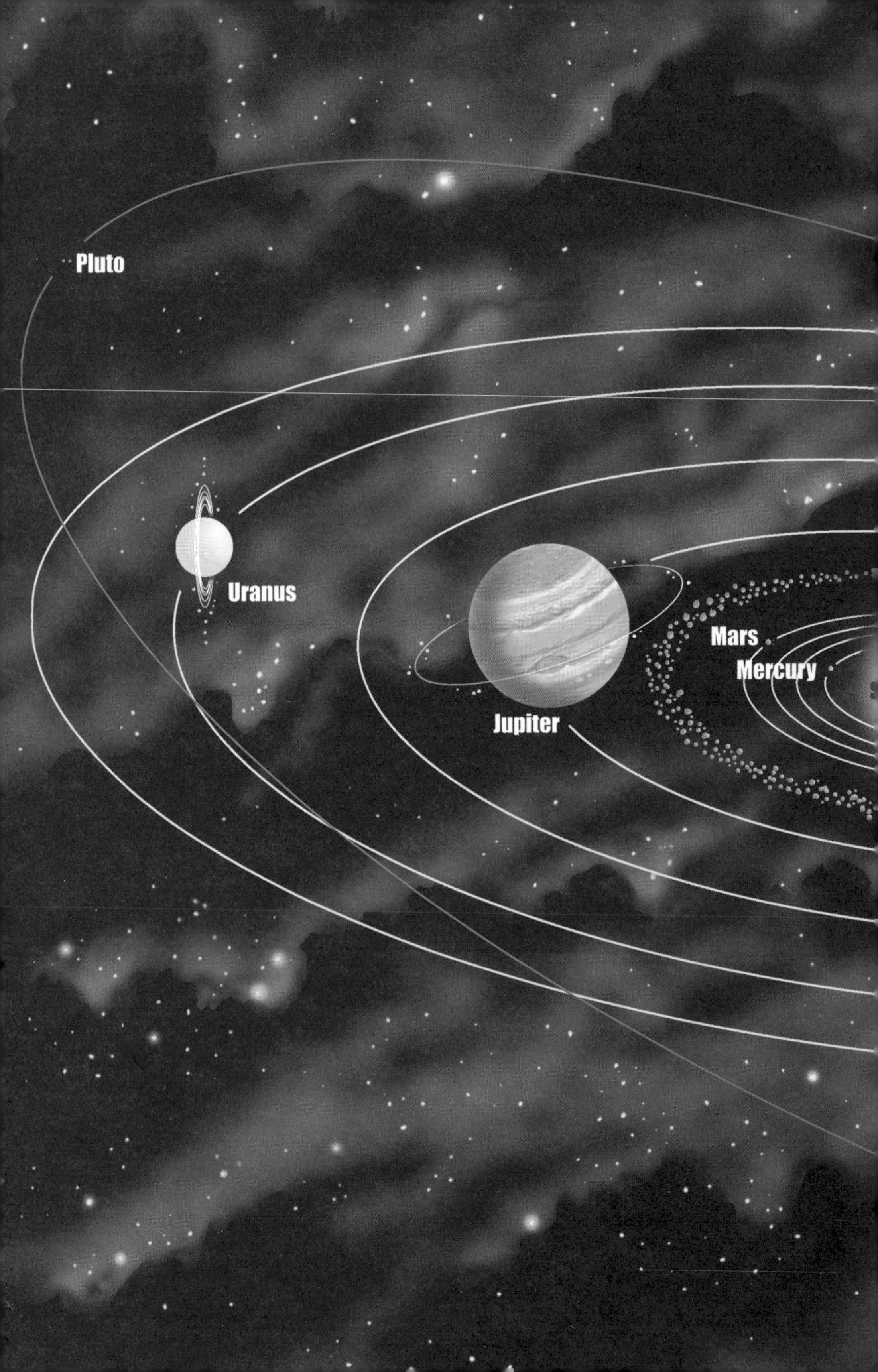
Pluto
Uranus
Jupiter
Mars
Mercury